The Trouble
with Samson

Written by Carol Jones

Illustrated by Martin Bailey

sundance

A Haights Cross Communications Company

a black dog book

Published by
Sundance Publishing
P.O. Box 1326
234 Taylor Street
Littleton, MA 01460

Copyright © text Carol Jones
Copyright © illustrations Martin Bailey

First published 2000 by
Pearson Education Australia Pty. Limited
95 Coventry Street
South Melbourne 3205 Australia
Exclusive United States Distribution: Sundance Publishing

Guided Reading Level I
Guided reading levels assigned by Sundance Publishing using the text characteristics
described by Fountas & Pinnell in the book *Guided Reading,* published by Heinemann.

ISBN 0-7608-5024-0

Contents

Characters

Sandy Grundy
is very bossy.

Candy Grundy is the
youngest in the family.

Andy Grundy wants
to be a surfer when
he grows up.

Samson is a very
shaggy dog who likes
to eat other people's food.

Chapter One
Problem Puppy

The Grundys had always wanted a dog.
Now they had Samson.
Samson played with Candy's toys. Candy
didn't mind the hairs on her teddy bear.
Andy was used to Samson's face
in his cornflakes.

But when the fleas moved
into Sandy's sock drawer,
enough was enough.
"That dog!" she said.
"Next he'll be wearing pants."

That night, the children waited
until Samson was watching TV.
Then they sneaked into the kitchen
for a family meeting.

"When we go surfing,
Samson hogs the surfboard," said Andy.

"When we play music,
Samson sings along," moaned Candy.

"The trouble is," said Sandy,

"that puppy thinks he's human."

"Something has to be done," they all said.

Chapter Two
Puppy School

home food

Andy, Sandy, and Candy tried to train
Samson. They threw sticks. But they were
the ones who had to fetch them.

Candy tried using a leash.

But she was the one who was led.

Andy even sent Samson to his doghouse.
But Samson howled so much that
Andy had to join him.

"I'll make a dog of him!" said Sandy
sternly. "I'll take him to puppy school."

At puppy school, the lessons for Samson
were how to sit and when to stay.
He was also shown how to walk
at Sandy's heel.

But when Samson sat, he wouldn't get up.
When he walked, he kept on walking.
Sandy was well trained, though!

Chapter Three
Camping Puppy

Andy had an idea.

"I'll make a dog of him," he said.

"I'll take him camping!"

Samson kept munching on corn chips.

Andy and Samson
waded through swamps.
They breathed the fresh air
and cooked over an open fire.

At bedtime, Samson slept on
the sleeping bag.
Poor Andy shivered by the fire.

When they got home,
Samson went in to watch TV.

"Poor Samson," said Candy.

"Maybe he just needs a friend."

Chapter Four
Stray Puppy

One day, Candy brought home a stray.
The kids smelled it before they saw it.

"What is it?" growled Sandy.

"It's a friend for Samson," said Candy.

Samson sniffed the stray
and stuck out his tongue.
Andy held his nose and opened the door.
"Don't come back!" he said.

Later, Candy put a bone
on the back steps.
But two bowls of dog food
and a pack of corn chips
were already there.
The stray was going to stay.

Chapter Five
Puppy Love

The next morning, Samson didn't eat
Andy's cornflakes.

He didn't go to school with Sandy.

He didn't follow Candy.

Instead, he went exploring with the stray.

No one knew where.

That night, Samson didn't finish dinner.

"Don't you want your ice cream?"
asked Andy.

There was no answer,
just a whiff of something yucky.

No more hairs on teddy bears.

No more whiskers in the cornflakes.

Instead, there were bones buried in pairs.

And chewed-up dolls in the backyard.